HOW TO THINK LIKE A SCIENTIST

Answering Questions by the Scientific Method

STEPHEN P. KRAMER
illustrated by Felicia Bond

HarperCollins*Publishers*

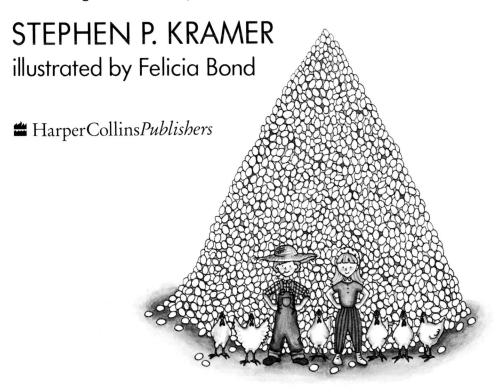

For Jeremy

With thanks to David Herbenson
for his advice and suggestions

How to Think Like a Scientist
Answering Questions by the Scientific Method
Text copyright © 1987 by Stephen P. Kramer
Illustrations copyright © 1987 by Felicia Bond

Library of Congress Cataloging-in-Publication Data
Kramer, Stephen P.
    How to think like a scientist.

    Summary: Uses questions about hypothetical situations
to introduce the process of thinking according to
scientific method.
    1. Science—Methodology—Juvenile literature.
[1. Science—Methodology]   I. Bond, Felicia, ill.
II. Title.
Q175.2.K73 1987   502.8   85-43604
ISBN 0-690-04563-8
ISBN 0-690-04565-4 (lib. bdg.)

21   23   25   27   29   30   28   26   24   22

Contents

HOW
TO THINK
LIKE
A SCIENTIST

"Whump, whump" went the tires of Pete's bike. The sounds were so close together they seemed like one noise.

"Hey!" screamed Pete. He pointed to the side of the road. "Look out! Get over!"

Jim could barely see the outline of Pete's arm in the darkness, but he swerved to the left. He coasted along the shoulder of the road until he caught up with Pete. Pete had stopped and was looking back.

"What's wrong?" asked Jim.

Pete shook his head. "A snake! A huge snake...I rode over it! On the side of the road! I didn't see it until too late...I couldn't even turn."

"Probably just an old inner tube," said Jim. "Come on, let's go."

"Was not," replied Pete, shaking his head again. "Want to go back and see?"

Jim hesitated for a moment. "All right," he answered. "I'm not scared."

Pete unhooked the flashlight from the frame of his bike. The boys laid their bicycles in the weeds beside the road and slowly walked back. The flashlight made a faint yellow spot on the pavement.

Pete shined the flashlight far ahead. "Up there," he said. "That's where I rode over it."

Jim looked around. "I don't see anything."

Pete shone the flashlight at the edge of the road. For a moment everything was still. Then, suddenly, the back half of a very large gopher snake disappeared into the roadside weeds.

Jim took a slow step backward. "You rode over that?"

Pete nodded. "I told you it wasn't an inner tube." He shone the flashlight directly on the spot where the snake had disappeared. "Think it's hurt?"

Jim shrugged. "It seems to be crawling all right."

"Maybe we should come back and look around tomorrow."

"OK," Jim agreed. "Let's wait until there's a little more light."

The boys turned and walked back to their bicycles. Pete kept the beam of light on the road.

"You know," said Jim, "my grandpa would call that a rain snake."

"What?" asked Pete.

"A rain snake. He'd say you could make it rain for sure with a snake like that."

"How?"

"Well," said Jim, "my grandpa grew up way back in the hills. When he was a boy, the farmers would sometimes use a dead snake to make it rain. They'd find a large tree with a strong low branch and throw the snake over the branch. A big snake like that would bring rain for sure."

Pete leaned over and picked up his bike. "You believe that?"

"Naw," answered Jim quickly. Then he scratched his head and looked back down the road. "But, well, I never tried it. I don't know. My grandpa says they did it a lot. Maybe it'd work for some people, sometimes...."

What do you think? Can throwing a dead snake over a tree branch bring rain?

Every day you answer questions—dozens or even hundreds of them. What should I wear today? What assignments do I need for school? Can I eat an extra piece of toast and still get to the bus on time? What should I do tonight?

Some questions you answer correctly. Others you don't. Some questions are important. You spend lots of time thinking about them. Other questions aren't important. You guess at the answer or just choose an answer automatically.

This book is about questions. It will show you how you usually answer questions, and why you sometimes get wrong answers. It will also show you how to use the scientific method. The scientific method can help you answer questions correctly.

In some ways this is like a book of riddles. You will be reading stories and parts of stories. Each story has a question. Some of the stories will show you how easy it is to answer questions incorrectly. Other stories show you how to find the correct answers to questions. Finally, there are a few questions that are left unanswered. If you're curious about any of them, you'll have to find the answers yourself.

Let's begin by telling some stories that show how you answer questions every day.

How
Do You Answer
Questions?

You think about many things when you try to answer a question. You try to remember things you know that might help you. You look for new information about the question. Sometimes you try to guess how someone else would answer the question. Other times you might pick an answer because of what you would *like* the answer to be. Sometimes these things help you find a correct answer. Other times they lead you to a wrong answer.

Here are three stories. Each story has a question. Each story tells about something that could happen to you, and each story will show a different way of answering a question.

Information

You're sitting on your bed one afternoon reading a book about a mountain climber. Things are getting very exciting (an avalanche has just started) when your little brother Ralphie walks into the room. He strolls past your bed and looks out the window.

"Hey," he says, "someone's in Mr. Murphy's backyard."

Your teeth start to grind. You've lost your place but you try not to show it. A long time ago you learned that sometimes the best way to get along with Ralphie is to ignore him.

"Hey," says Ralphie, "they're going into the Murphys' house."

You frown and roll over, wondering when Ralphie is going to go away.

"Hey," says Ralphie, "they're coming out of the Murphys' house. They're carrying something that's all covered up. They're stealing something from the Murphys!"

You sit up straight. The Murphys? Someone is stealing something from the Murphys?

QUESTION: Is someone stealing something from the Murphys?

Then, out the window you see a truck. It is parked in front of the Murphys' house. Painted in large blue letters on the side of the truck are the words "Jake's TV Repair."

You shake your head.

"Go on," you tell Ralphie. "Take off."

"They're stealing something from the Murphys' house," says Ralphie. "The bad man just went back inside."

"It's not a bad man," you explain. "Someone's just picking up the TV. Can't you see that truck out there?"

"They're not taking the TV," Ralphie insists.

"Get out!" you shout.

"No!" says Ralphie.

"I said get out!" you scream, throwing a pillow at Ralphie.

So Ralphie finally leaves, walking out of the room very slowly.

That night at dinner the telephone rings. Your father answers it. When he returns to the table, he says, "The Murphys just got home. While they were gone this afternoon, someone broke into their house and stole some money. The burglars also took some silverware and Mr. Murphy's violin.

"Most of our neighbors were gone this afternoon. The Johnsons didn't see anything because they were watching a repairman fix their TV all afternoon. Did any of you see anything?"

Ralphie sits up straight and begins nodding.

What happened? The question was: Is someone stealing something from the Murphys? You and Ralphie both made observations. Ralphie's observations told him the answer was *yes*. Your observations told you the answer was *no*. Why did you and Ralphie end up with different answers to the same question?

You answered the question incorrectly because of the way you used an observation. You saw a TV repair truck through the front window. Your observation was a good one. You noticed what kind of truck was on your street and where it was parked. The problem was how you used your observation. You thought the truck was giving you information about who was in the Murphys' house. Actually, Ralphie was giving you better information.

Information must be used carefully. Having information does not always mean you will answer a question correctly. If the information is not true or is not used in the right way, it can lead to a wrong answer.

What Other People Say

Sometimes we answer questions in a certain way because of what other people think or say. Here's another story.

It's Wednesday morning, just before lunch. Your teacher

arranged for someone from the zoo to come and show your class some animals. You have seen an iguana, a mongoose, and a large snake. Now the zookeeper reaches into a wooden box and pulls out a fishbowl. He sets the bowl on a low table at the front of the room. Three small gray fish swim back and forth.

"Who knows the name of these fish?" asks the zookeeper.

Everyone is quiet. You stare at the fish for a moment. Of course

you know what they are. They're guppies! They look just like the fish in your sister's aquarium. You've spent hours watching guppies.

Quickly, you raise your hand, but you're sitting in the last row and the zookeeper doesn't see you.

You wave your hand back and forth. The girl next to you ducks.

"These are gastromorphs," says the zookeeper. "They live in slow, muddy streams in Africa. They are very dangerous. They will eat almost anything that moves."

Quickly, you pull your hand down and look around. "Whew," you think. "That could have been embarrassing." Then you lean forward and squint at those fish again.

"We always keep a strong screen over this fishbowl when we visit schools. If anyone were to stick a hand in the water, well, these little fish would immediately attack and begin taking bites out of it."

QUESTION: What kind of fish is in the bowl?

This time the question seems easy. The fish look a lot like guppies. They swim like guppies. They're even the size and color of guppies. But would you stick your hand in the bowl? Of course not! The zookeeper just told you they are gastromorphs. Zookeepers know their animals, right? So the fish must be gastromorphs. Maybe.

Here's what really happened. The zookeeper who was supposed to visit your class got sick. The zoo sent over the person who normally takes care of birds. The zookeeper who came to your class knew a lot about birds, but not much about fish.

His first stop that morning was at the mammal house to pick up the mongoose. Then he went to the reptile house to get the iguana and the snake. He took all three animals with him into the fish house.

It was dark in the fish house. All the fish were arranged alphabetically in separate aquariums. The guppies were in the aquarium next to the gastromorphs. The zookeeper picked up a net, walked over to the gastromorphs, and leaned over the aquarium to dip some out. Just then the snake began to crawl out of its bag, so the zookeeper reached down to push it back in. When he stood up straight again he had three fish in his net. He dumped them into the fishbowl and hurried to your school. What he didn't know was that he had accidentally dipped the net into the wrong tank. He had netted three guppies instead of three gastromorphs.

You really were right! The fish were guppies, but you changed your mind because of what the zookeeper said.

Sometimes other people are wrong. Usually zookeepers know much more about animals than you do, but maybe not every time. If you answer questions by depending too much on other people's answers, you probably will make mistakes.

Because We Want To

Sometimes we know how we would like a question to be answered. We choose an answer to a question because it's the answer we like. Let's look at another story.

It's Friday afternoon, and the last bell of the day has just rung. You gather up your books and start toward the door of your classroom. As you step into the hallway your teacher calls out, "Don't forget to finish your math assignment. It's due Monday morning." You look down and check to be sure you have your math book.

The weekend passes quickly. On Friday night you go to a basketball game. On Saturday your family goes to the beach. Finally, on Sunday evening you clear a spot on the kitchen table and start to work on your assignment.

Just then the telephone rings. You hurry to answer it.

"Hi," says Pat. "What are you doing?"

"Math," you answer.

"Hey," says Pat, "I've got a better idea. There's a good movie downtown. My dad gave me some money. Let's go."

"I can't," you answer. "I haven't even started this assignment yet."

"It's a great movie," says Pat. "Everyone says so."

"Look, report cards are coming out next week. I need a good grade on this paper."

"It's the last chance," says Pat. "They're changing movies tomorrow."

"Well…" You're having a terrible time deciding what to do. Then you suddenly remember something!

"Maybe we won't have to turn in this paper tomorrow. We haven't even graded Thursday's paper yet."

"That's right," says Pat.

You take a deep breath. All you can think about is how much you want to see the movie. "And Ms. Wilson does forget to collect papers sometimes. Remember last Monday's assignment? It was Wednesday before she collected it."

"Right!" says Pat. "I'll tell you what," he continues. "As soon as the bell rings on Monday, I'll ask her what she did this weekend. She'll forget all about the assignment."

"OK," you answer. "I'll be right over."

H.C. STORM SCHOOL

QUESTION: Is Ms. Wilson going to collect the math assignment Monday morning?

On Monday morning, just as the bell finishes ringing, Pat asks the question. "Ms. Wilson, did you have a nice weekend?"

"Why, thank you, Pat," she replies. "I did have a nice weekend. On Friday night I went to a movie and on Saturday I went canoeing."

Pat looks over at you and grins.

15

"I'll tell you all about it," continues Ms. Wilson, "while you're passing your math papers up to the front of the room."

Suddenly you feel very sick.

You were sure the answer to the question would be "no." You didn't think the papers would be collected, but you were wrong. As a matter of fact, you are the only person in the whole class who doesn't have the paper finished. What happened?

Part of the reason you answered the question incorrectly was because of an observation. You remembered that another paper due on Monday wasn't collected until later. But another reason you answered the question incorrectly was that you didn't *want* the paper to be collected. You convinced yourself it wouldn't be collected on Monday morning because you wanted to go to a movie instead of finishing the assignment.

Sometimes we really want the answer to a question to turn out in a certain way. Such a question can be difficult to answer correctly or fairly. Often it is easier to find an answer we like than an answer that is correct.

Carelessly used information, what others think, what we want to happen—none of these are very reliable ways of answering questions. Too many times they lead to wrong answers. Is there a better way? How can you find out whether throwing a dead snake over a tree branch really will bring rain?

Using the Scientific Method

Scientists are people who are curious. They want to know about the things around them. They are always asking questions and trying to answer them.

Some scientists study birds. They might ask the question, "Why do meadowlarks sing?" Other scientists study objects in the universe. They might ask, "What happens to stars as they grow older?" Other scientists might ask: "What are atoms made of?" "How does gravity work?" "What lives at the bottom of the ocean?" "Why does the wind blow?" "How does the body heal itself?" Still other scientists might be interested in learning about old folktales and checking to see if any of them are true. Such a scientist might be interested in the question, "Can throwing a dead snake over a tree branch bring rain?"

Scientists believe that the things around us behave in certain ways. They believe that things that happen can be described by certain rules. Scientists try to find patterns in things. They look for explanations for the patterns in the things around us.

Scientists learn about things by observing and measuring them. Science can deal only with things that can be observed. To a scientist, being able to observe something means that we can learn about it by using our senses. It can be seen, heard, smelled, touched, or tasted.

Scientists often use instruments to help them make observations. Machines and special instruments can tell us much about things we can't know by using our senses alone. But if there is no way to observe and measure something, it can't be studied scientifically.

Questions are important to scientists. Scientists use questions to learn about things. Scientists are careful about how they answer questions. They know it is easy to answer questions incorrectly. Scientists know about the problems of observing things carefully. They also know it is easy to be influenced by what they want to happen and by what others think.

It is sometimes hard to explain exactly how a scientist answers a question. It may seem to happen by accident in a laboratory one day. It might happen after a thousand careful experiments. Or a scientist might think of the correct answer one afternoon while riding the bus home from work.

Scientists who "suddenly" find the answer to a question usually have been thinking about the question for a long time. They may have done many experiments to give them clues about the correct answer. Scientists use a series of steps to make answering questions easier. The steps also help scientists make sure answers are correct.

These five steps are called the scientific method:

1. Ask a question.
2. Gather information about the question.
3. Form a hypothesis.
4. Test the hypothesis.
5. Tell others what you found.

Let's make up another story. The story has a question. We'll use the steps of the scientific method to answer the question.

Suppose you moved to the country and bought a chicken farm. For a whole year you fed chickens, cleaned their cages, counted eggs, and watched baby chicks grow.

After a year you got tired of chickens. All the clucking and crowing was bothering you, and the feathers were making you sneeze. You decided to take a one-month vacation. Another farmer who lived nearby agreed to take care of your chickens while you were gone.

When you returned from your vacation, you checked the records. You were surprised to learn that while you were away, your hens had laid twice as many eggs as usual. You would probably be curious about why your hens had laid so many eggs.

QUESTION: Why did the hens lay more eggs
            while you were gone?

1. The first step of the scientific method is to ask a question. Maybe you have noticed several differences in your chickens since you returned. Perhaps they are noisier than when you left. Perhaps they also seem fatter, or thinner, or crabbier. If your chickens are now fatter and crabbier than when you left, maybe it's for the same reason they are laying more eggs.

But maybe not. Maybe they are fatter for one reason, crabbier for another reason, and laying more eggs for still another reason. Scientists usually try to work on one question at a time. The question you are trying to answer is, "Why did the hens lay more eggs while I was gone?"

2. The next step is to gather information that might help you answer the question. You search for clues, just as a detective would. Your job is to find things that might explain why the hens laid more eggs. Was the weather any different while you were gone? Were other farmers' hens laying more eggs than usual too? Did the other farmer take care of your chickens differently from the way you do?

You could start by talking to other people. The local weather bureau could provide information about last month's weather. Other chicken farmers could tell you if their hens had been laying more eggs than usual.

If the weather hadn't changed much and other hens had been laying their usual number of eggs, you might want to talk to the farmer who took care of your chickens. You could ask him exactly what he'd done.

Suppose the farmer said, "I fed your hens and gave them fresh water every morning. You had only one small water dish in each pen. The water dishes were usually empty in the mornings. I didn't think your hens were getting enough water, so I replaced the small water dishes with larger ones. The large dishes held enough water to last through the day.

"I collected eggs every morning. I also cleaned the pens every other day. You know, you didn't leave nearly enough chicken feed. It ran out right after you left, so I gave your hens my Acme Deluxe Chicken Feed."

Now, look carefully at what the farmer told you. You are trying to discover exactly what he did. Were there any differences in the way he took care of your chickens? It might help to make a table like this:

What happened to the chickens during vacation	The same way you take care of chickens	Different from the way you take care of chickens
1. Fed and given fresh water every morning	X	
2. Had large water dishes		X
3. Eggs collected every morning	X	
4. Pens cleaned every other day	X	
5. Fed Acme Deluxe Chicken Feed		X

The table makes it easy to see what happened. Many of the things the other farmer did were the same as what you do. However, while you were gone the hens had larger water dishes. Also, for most of the vacation they ate a different kind of chicken feed.

3. Now you are ready to form a hypothesis. A hypothesis is a guess that is based on observations. You have already discovered that the other farmer gave your hens larger water dishes. Perhaps the extra water helped them lay more eggs. You might guess, "Giving my hens more water causes them to lay more eggs." Such a guess is called a hypothesis.

4. The next step is to find out whether or not your guess is correct. It is called testing the hypothesis. You will need to do an experiment to help you decide whether the hypothesis is true. If it is true, you have answered the question about why your hens laid more eggs. If it is not true, you will have to think of another hypothesis to test.

Scientists need to be careful about how they plan their experiments. They must be sure they are testing the right hypothesis. They must also be sure they are using the information from the experiment in the right way.

Let's examine an experiment. Pretend that you do the following things:

A. Keep large water dishes in each chicken pen. Now the hens will have as much water as they did while you were gone.

B. Take care of the hens exactly the way you did before you left on vacation. Don't change anything that you were doing.

1. Feed the hens and give them fresh water every morning.
2. Use your regular chicken feed.
3. Clean the pens every other day.
4. Collect eggs every morning.

C. Compare the number of eggs the hens lay now to how many they laid before vacation.

What could this experiment tell you? Suppose the hens begin laying lots of eggs. Suppose they are laying two or even three times as many eggs as they had before vacation. It must be because of the extra water, right?

Maybe, but maybe not. Perhaps there is another explanation.

27

Your hens might be laying more eggs now for a completely different reason.

What if the weather has suddenly gotten warm, and the change in weather is causing your hens to lay more eggs?

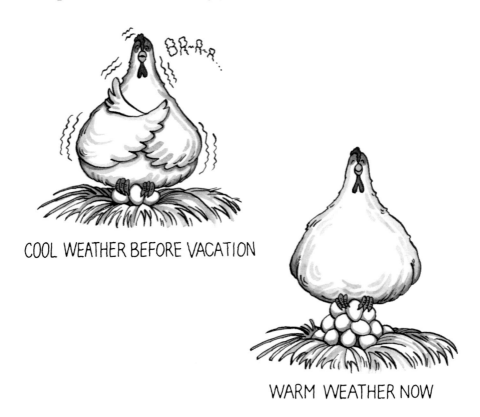

COOL WEATHER BEFORE VACATION

WARM WEATHER NOW

What if the sun hatched thousands of grasshopper eggs last week? Maybe hundreds of baby grasshoppers are leaping into the chicken pens and your hens are gobbling them up. Perhaps the extra food is causing them to lay more eggs.

GRASSHOPPER SUPPLY
BEFORE VACATION

GRASSHOPPER SUPPLY NOW

Maybe if the hens are laying more eggs now, it's not because of the extra water at all. Perhaps it's for a completely different reason. But how can you tell? The experiment you did cannot help you decide.

Scientists have a better way of doing the experiment. If the experiment is changed, it can help you decide why the hens are laying more eggs. The experiment is done with two groups. One is called the control group. The other is the experimental group. The two groups are treated almost exactly the same. The experiment will work only if almost everything about the groups is the same. For example, to do the experiment with your hens you would have to:

CONTROL GROUP   EXPERIMENTAL GROUP

1. Use the same number of hens in each group.

2. Use hens that are all about the same size and age.

3. Give all hens the same amount of chicken feed at the same time of day.

4. Give all hens the same kind of chicken feed.

5. Let all hens have the same amount of exercise.

6. Put all hens in the same kind of pen. Be sure the pens are in places where the light and temperature will be the same.

Your hypothesis is, "Giving my hens extra water causes them to lay more eggs." You could test your hypothesis by doing the following experiment. Give one group of hens the same amount of water you always did (use small water dishes). Give the other group of hens more water (use large water dishes). The first group is the control group. The second is the experimental group. Except for the amount of water provided, everything about the two groups remains the same.

Count the number of eggs laid by each group for one week. Continue counting the eggs every week for five weeks. Examine your results.

CONTROL GROUP   EXPERIMENTAL GROUP

1. Give the hens in the control-group pens small water dishes. Give the hens in the experimental-group pens large water dishes. Provide *all* the hens with fresh water in their dishes every morning, just as you have always done.

2. Count the number of eggs laid by each group for a week.

3. Continue the experiment for a total of five weeks.

Dividing your hens into two groups that are observed at the same time makes your experiment better. You can be more certain that any differences in egg laying are caused by the amount of water the hens have. If weather makes a difference in egg laying, both groups should be affected in the same way. If baby grasshoppers start hatching and jumping into the pens, both groups should be affected. If exercise makes a difference, again, both groups should react in the same way.

What if the hens in the experimental group laid a lot more eggs than those in the control group during every week of the experiment? Then you could be pretty sure it was because they were getting extra water. You have tried to keep everything else about the groups the same.

What if the control group produced about the same number of eggs as the experimental group? Or what if sometimes the control group produced more eggs and sometimes the experimental group produced more eggs? Then the amount of water doesn't seem to be making any difference. You would have to reject your hypothesis and try a new one.

Sometimes it is hard to decide what the results of an experiment mean. If the experimental group laid more eggs during each of the five weeks, you could be pretty sure the water was making a difference. If the experimental group laid more eggs for four out of five weeks, you might still be pretty sure the water was making a difference. But what if the experimental group laid more eggs only three out of five weeks? Maybe the water isn't making any difference. Maybe if you did the entire experiment again, the experimental group would lay more eggs only two weeks out of five.

Scientists can use a type of mathematics called statistics to help them decide what the results of an experiment mean. Statistics can help a scientist in planning an experiment. Statistics can also help a scientist decide whether the results of an experiment support a hypothesis or not.

If a hypothesis seems to be true, a scientist will often repeat the experiment. The scientist may do the experiment many times to make sure the result is always the same. Other scientists often also repeat another scientist's important experiment.

If the amount of water didn't seem to make any difference in the number of eggs laid, you would have to try a new hypothesis. You know that your hens ate a different kind of chicken feed most of the time you were on vacation. You might decide to test the hypothesis, "My hens will lay more eggs if they eat Acme Deluxe Chicken Feed instead of the feed I usually give them."

CONTROL GROUP:
regular food

EXPERIMENTAL GROUP:
different food

You could set up another experiment using control and experimental groups. The only difference between the two groups would be that they would get different kinds of chicken feed. The control group would get the kind of chicken feed you usually use. The experimental group would get Acme Deluxe Chicken Feed. If you did the experiment several times, the number of eggs produced by each group would help you decide whether the second hypothesis was true or false.

5. Finally, an important part of the scientific method is telling other people what you learned. A chicken farmer who suddenly discovers how to make his hens lay more eggs might not be anxious to share his secret. After all, he's trying to make a living from selling eggs and would like to be able to sell them more cheaply than anyone else.

However, a scientist who discovered how to make hens lay more eggs would write about his findings. His discovery might appear in a magazine called a scientific journal. Scientific journals print news about scientists' experiments and hypotheses.

Scientists answer questions and learn new things every day. No one could ever read or remember all the things scientists have discovered. Scientists who study fish can read journals that print articles about fish. Scientists who study plants or rocks or atoms can read journals about the things they study. Reading journals teaches scientists many things. It helps them improve their own experiments. It also gives them ideas about new things to study.

What Do You Want to Know?

Now that you know how the scientific method works, you can probably think of some questions it could help you answer. Perhaps you have a younger brother. You know that he is much harder to get along with when he misses his afternoon nap. But what is it about his behavior that makes him harder to get along with? How does he act differently? Let's use the steps of the scientific method to see how you could find the answer.

1. *Ask a question.*

How does my little brother act differently when he misses his afternoon nap?

2. *Gather information about the question.*

Watch your brother on days when he takes a nap and on days when he misses his nap. Ask your parents or brothers or sisters how he acts differently.

36

3. *Form a hypothesis.*

"My little brother has less patience in the evenings on days he misses his nap than on days he takes a nap."

4. *Test the hypothesis.*

Perhaps you've noticed that some evenings your little brother will work for a long time putting the pieces of a puzzle together. Other times he gets mad at the puzzle and throws the pieces across the room. You might decide to measure your brother's patience by checking how long he will work on putting together a puzzle.

a. Pick five days when your brother takes a nap. After dinner on those days give him a puzzle to put together. Count how many pieces he uses before giving up. This is the control group.

b. Pick five days when your brother misses his nap. After dinner on those days give him a puzzle to put together. Count how many pieces he uses before giving up. This is the experimental group.

◄ CONTROL GROUP
5 days with a nap

EXPERIMENTAL GROUP ▶
5 days without a nap

Of course, you would have to use puzzles that were all about the same difficulty. You would also have to be careful not to use one puzzle too many times, or your brother might begin to put it together more easily than the others.

However, if you did have enough puzzles, you could probably get a good idea of how much patience your brother had each evening. If your brother always put together more of the puzzle after taking a nap, he might also be more patient and easier to get along with.

What if the results of your experiment don't support your hypothesis? Perhaps the number of puzzle pieces your brother puts together is not really a good measure of his patience. You might try to think of another way to measure how much patience he has.

If there is no evidence from any of your experiments to support your hypothesis, try a different one. A hypothesis you could test quite easily would be, "My brother cries more often in the evenings on days when he misses his nap."

> **a.** Pick five days when your brother takes a nap. Count the number of times he cries between 6:00 P.M. and 8:00 P.M. This is the control group.

> **b.** Pick five days when your brother misses his nap. Count the number of times he cries between 6:00 P.M. and 8:00 P.M. This is the experimental group.

Examine your results. Does your brother really seem to cry more in the evenings on days when he misses his nap?

5. *Tell someone what you found.*

Your parents might be interested. Your older brother or sister might like to know. What you learned might make babysitting easier.

Everywhere you look there are questions you could use the scientific method to answer.

Which kind of food does your dog like best?

Does your mother go to bed earlier on weekday nights or on weekend nights?

Do you eat more food on days when you go to school or on days when you stay home?

Does your father drive the car more on weekdays or on weekends?

Do dishes really get cleaner if you wash them in hot water instead of cold water?

Is your older sister more likely to help you if you say please?

There are thousands of questions you can ask and answer. You might learn some surprising things. You might learn something your parents or teachers didn't know. You might even learn something no one else ever knew. That's what makes science exciting. There are all kinds of new discoveries to be made. All you have to do is ask the right question—and know how to answer it.

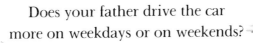

What
Do You
Think?

We've looked at quite a few stories. There have been many questions and answers. You know that a burglar did take some things from the Murphys' house. You also know that the zookeeper brought guppies instead of gastromorphs and that Ms. Wilson doesn't always forget to collect math assignments on Monday mornings. But what about snakes and rain? Can throwing a dead snake over a tree branch bring rain?

Scientists have learned a lot about weather in the last hundred years. They have found that wind patterns, the amount of moisture in the air, and warm and cold air masses all affect rainfall.

A good scientist is skeptical. "How could throwing a dead snake over a tree branch bring rain?" the scientist would ask. "Can it change wind patterns? Can it change air temperature? Can it make warm or cold air masses move in different directions?"

"Of course not!" you're probably thinking. "I guess that answers the question. Throwing a dead snake over a tree branch couldn't possibly bring rain."

Except…

Besides being skeptical, a good scientist always has an open mind. Good scientists don't always believe something is true or false because of what others say. They know how easy it is to be wrong. And they know that sometimes experiments show us surprising things.

Of course, no one is telling you to go outside and find a snake to kill. The kinds of places snakes like to live are disappearing too fast. The snakes you see deserve to be protected and left alone.

Suppose you were riding your bicycle along a country road late one afternoon. Suppose you found a snake that had been killed by a car, but not too badly squashed. Suppose you scooped it into an empty plastic bag and tied the top of the bag in a tight knot. Suppose you put that bag into another plastic bag and sealed it tightly too. And suppose you found a nice spot way in the back of the freezer where you could keep the snake awhile, a place where your mother would never find it.

Well, with that snake and what you know about the scientific method, you could answer the question about dead snakes, tree branches, and rain all by yourself.

Index